SEASONS OF THE HEART

SEASONS OF THE HEART

The Spiritual Dynamic of the Carmelite Life

John Welch, O.Carm.

Carmelite Media

Darien, Illinois

Cover design by Sister Catherine Martin, O.Carm.

Copyright 2008 by John Welch, O.Carm.
Second Printing, 2009

Library of Congress Cataloging-in-Publication Data

Welch, John, 2008-
        Seasons of the Heart

ISBN-13: 9780615232768
ISBN-10:   06152327611

Published by Carmelite Media
8501 Bailey Road, Darien, Illinois

Printed and bound in the United States of America

*The material in this booklet was first presented
during a day of recollection for the delegates
at a General Chapter of the Carmelite Order.*

*Sr. Catherine Martin, O.Carm., has provided imagery, and
reflections, to accompany the text. Sr. Catherine, a member
of the Congregation of Our Lady of Mount Carmel,
works in a studio in Lafayette, Louisiana.*

TABLE OF CONTENTS

SEASONS OF THE HEART

John Welch, O.Carm.

The Spiritual Dynamic of the Carmelite Life

Introduction

The Carmelite tradition could be understood as an 800 year commentary on the *Song of Songs*. This ancient love story in Hebrew scripture is a basic narrative capturing the experience of countless Carmelites. *"The voice of my beloved! Look, he comes, leaping upon the mountains, bounding over the hills."* (2,8) Thinking they were seeking an elusive God, they returned from their search with the conviction that God had been pursuing them all along in love. The yearning deep within the heart of the Carmelite has been revealed as the trace of an invitation, *"Arise my love, my fair one, and come away."* (2,10)

Carmelite writers have frequently turned to the passionate love story of the *Song of Songs* for words to meet their experience. John of the Cross drew on the story and images of the *Song* for his love poem *The Spiritual Canticle*. Teresa of Avila wrote a commentary on the *Song*. And Thérèse of Lisieux identified with its story but, unlike the waiting lover in the *Song*, Thérèse said she always found the Beloved in her bed.

Whether consciously referring to the *Song* or not, its lines can be found in Carmelite stories. Carmelites tell many stories, but the story of the lover restlessly awaiting the approach of the Beloved emerges as a common theme. Their union in love and their retreat into the solitude of high mountain pastures finds equivalent expression in the stories of Carmelites. John of the Cross found Hosea's words expressive of his experience, *"...I will now allure her, and bring her into the wilderness, and speak tenderly to her."* (2,14) Responding to an invitation from a mysterious Presence met within searching lives, Carmelites have been drawn into a relationship which forever changes them: *"...the winter is past, the rain is over and gone. The flowers appear on the earth; the time of singing has come..."* (2, 11-12)

Fundamental themes of Carmelite spirituality emerge in this story of the human heart. These themes reveal a spiritual dynamism at the core of Carmelite life which can be described as *"seasons of the heart."* The intent of this discussion is to review these "seasons of the heart" in an attempt identify the spiritual dynamic of the Carmelite life.

There are five *"seasons"* identified in this discussion:

- A LONGING HEART (our desire for God)
- AN ENSLAVED HEART (the worship of false gods)
- A LISTENING HEART (contemplative prayer)
- A TROUBLED HEART (the tragic in life)
- A PURE HEART (the transformation of desire).
- Endnotes

These *"seasons of the heart,"* and Carmel's expression of them, are among the realities which gave rise to the Carmelite tradition, establishing it as one of the major spiritual paths for Christians.

A LONGING HEART
Our desire for God

We choose all

"Our hearts are restless," wrote St. Augustine, and that truth remains fundamental to the human condition. Human restlessness, human desire, human yearning – none of it ever seems finally and fully satisfied. The baby beginning to crawl and explore the environment is an expression of human restlessness; the journeying of the first Carmelites who left their homes to gather in a valley on Mount Carmel was fueled by the same desire. We are truly pilgrims.

We humans never have enough because, with St. Thérèse of Lisieux, we choose all. And we will never rest until we get it. The Carmelite tradition recognizes this hunger in the human heart and says we are made this way. We are made to seek and search, to yearn and ache, until the heart finally finds something or someone to match the depth of its desire, until the heart finds food sufficient for its hunger. We name that food, that fulfilment, that goal of human desire, God. Carmelites have been intentionally pursuing that elusive, mysterious fulfilment for 800 years. *"I wanted to live,"* wrote St. Teresa of Avila, *"but I had no one to give me life..."* (1)

We believe that, named or not, every human being is on this quest. We can assume this: that every student in our school, every member of our parish, every pilgrim to our shrine, every candidate in our seminary has an openness to the transcendent mystery we name God. Time and time again the desire will be denied, the hunger temporarily satisfied, the yearning stifled, distracted, weak. But we know it is there and it will emerge in one form or another. Our tradition has the power, the language, the imagery to help illumine what people are experiencing in their innermost being.

The Carmelite tradition attempts to name the hunger, give words to the desire, and express the journey's end in God. The human heart will forever need this clarification of its wants. Carmel has wanted the same thing and will walk with anyone who is met along the way. We cannot satisfy their hunger, but can help them find words for it and know where it points. We can do it, and have done it, in art, in poetry and song, in counseling and teaching, in simply listening and understanding. And we can warn people that eventually all words fail and at times all we have is the desire itself.

One contemporary author observes that a serious problem in spirituality today is a naiveté about the desire or energy that drives us. Our God-given spiritual longing, which may be expressed in numerous ways, including creative, erotic energy, is dangerous for us if not carefully tended. We are naive about this deep desire within us and are not alert to its danger. Without a reverence toward this energy and ways of accessing it and keeping it contained, most adults waver between alienation from this fire and therefore live in depression, or allow themselves to be consumed by it and live in a state of inflation.

Depression, in this sense, means the inability to take child-like delight in life, to feel true joy. Inflation refers to our tendency, at times, to identify with this fire, this power of the gods. "…We are generally so full of ourselves that we are a menace to our families, friends, communities, and ourselves." Unable to handle this energy we either feel dead inside or are hyperactive and restless. *"Spirituality is about finding the proper ways, disciplines, by which to both access that energy and contain it."* (2)

Desires of the Carmelites

This dilemma would be understood by the saints of Carmel, They approached this flame found deep in their humanity and were burned and purified by it in their encounter. Teresa of Avila understood it as the water Jesus offered the Samaritan woman. More fire than water, it increases one's desire. *"How thirsty one becomes for this thirst!"* (3) John of the Cross begins his poem The Spiritual Canticle by complaining, *"Where have you hidden, Beloved, and left me moaning? You fled like the stag after wounding me; I went out calling you, but you were gone."* (4) John's understanding of our humanity is that we wake up in the middle of a love story. Someone has touched our hearts, wounding them, and making them ache for fulfilment. Who has done this to us, and where has that one gone? Those questions haunt every human being's journey, and propel every step from the crawling of a baby, to a Pope's pilgrimage to the Holy Land, and all the human endeavor in-between.

John complained that our desires are like little children. We pay attention to them and they settle down for a while. But soon they are up and noisily disrupting the peace of the house. Or, our desires are like a longed-for day with a loved one; but the day turns out to be a big disappointment! John's understanding of our humanity is that we have a hunger for which only God is sufficient food.

Thérèse of Lisieux found her deepest desires captured by the image of heaven: heaven as the never-ending Sunday, the eternal retreat, the eternal shore. The eternal shore is a particularly. evocative expression holding her heart's yearning. She chose all in life, and this image for her is an expression of all that she desires. But no image or concept fully expresses her longings:

> *"I feel how powerless I am to express in human language the secrets of heaven, and after writing page upon page I find that I have not yet begun. There are so many different horizons, so many nuances of infinite variety..."* (SS. 189)

We reach out to this and that, lured by a promise of fulfilment, but only to be disappointed time and time again. Using Thérèse's image, we arrive at many shores, but each time we realize it is not the eternal shore.

Spirit and psyche inhabit the same country of the mind. Spirit is the dynamism in us to fullness of being, to knowing all, loving all, being one with all. Psyche expresses these desires with primordial images drawn from the body, from the earth. Psyche connects the organism of the body and its rootedness in the cosmos with the transcendence of spirit and its yearning for fullness. Our images of hope, such as of *eternal shore*, express both psyche and spirit.

Psyche's images are freighted with spirit's yearnings. They may stir up and express our longings for peace and justice, they may open us to profound repentance, they may throw light on our existence and illumine our path, they may provide hopeful scenarios of our future beyond this life, as Thérèse's did. But, none of them is adequate to finally and fully express the desires within us, the desire that we are. Our deepest yearning to know and to love, to be one with, all there is, is never fulfilled. Our deepest hungers never find sufficient food in this life. Our wants are given voice, but what do we want?

Theologian Bernard Lonergan believed that if we follow the trail of our deepest desires, expressing them in truth, facing them, and responding to their call in our lives, we will undergo conversions. Our wants, our desires will be purified and transformed, until more and more we want what God wants in a consonance of desire.

What do the men and women in our parishes, our retreat houses, in counseling want? Everything! Count on it, and minister to it. And we say to ourselves and them, that the hunger within us is so deep and powerful that, acknowledged or not, only God is sufficient food. When Jesus preached the present and coming Reign of God he was speaking precisely to the deep desires, the holy longing in the hearts of his listeners.

March 24, 2005 was the 25th anniversary of the assassination of Archbishop Oscar Romero in San Salvador. He was killed while celebrating Eucharist in a Carmelite chapel. Romero's conversion from a rather traditional, professional cleric with a sincere but otherworldly piety, to an outspoken courageous shepherd of his people, came because he saw the longing in the faces of his people. As he celebrated the funerals of those killed by the powerful, and read off the names of the disappeared, he found it was his duty more and more to give voice to these voiceless ones, to express their oppressed longings – to embody in his courageous presence the holy longing of the Salvadoran people.

To assist people in hearing and voicing their deepest longing is part of Carmel's continuing ministry. The first Carmelites established conditions in their small valley which would bring order to their multiple desires. Each inhabited a cell and the cells surrounded a chapel, in which they daily remembered God's desire for them. Teresa of Avila founded enclosed communities within which the women could open themselves to the full force of their desires in affectionate friendship with the Lord and one another. She encouraged them to follow the lure of their depths as their fragmented desires found healing and reorientation. Both she and Thérèse believed firmly that if God has given us such longings God will ultimately fulfill them. We are not a useless passion.

Summary

Our Carmelite tradition acknowledges the hunger for God deep in the human heart. This yearning or longing propels us through our lives as we seek a fulfilment of our heart's desire. This deep current of desire within our lives is the result of God having first desired us. God, the first contemplative, gazed on us and made us lovable, and alluring to God. The Carmelite tradition does not speak of an annihilation of desire, but a *transformation* of desire so that more and more we desire what God desires in a consonance of desire. As Teresa of Avila said simply, *now I want what You want.*

Questions for reflection

- How do I experience this longing, this hunger, which is ultimately for God? Am I aware of a fundamental disease, a restlessness? Can I find places in my life where this yearning is expressing itself?

- What gives me deepest joy and delight in life? When do I feel the most creative and alive? Do I push away, ignore, or suppress it, or do I find ways of honoring this fire within me?

- How do I give expression to my deepest longings? What activity embodies them and keeps me hungering for their ultimate fulfilment?

- How do the people, among whom I minister, express their deepest yearning, their hearts' desires? How do I, with them, find the language for this yearning, and celebrate it as gift which points to God?

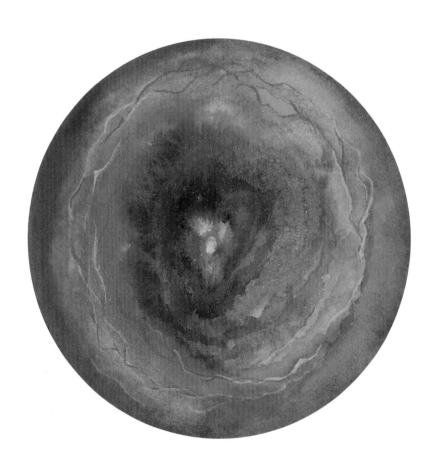

AN ENSLAVED HEART
The worship of false gods

Settling down with idols

A second perennial theme in Carmel's spirituality is the need to decide which God to follow. Our tradition was born on Mount Carmel, the scene of the struggle between the followers of Yahweh and the followers of Baal. Elijah encouraged the people to be clear about their choice of the one, true God. The Carmelite community as well as individual Carmelites have had to continually wrestle with the forces of disintegration and fragmentation brought about by the pursuit of idols.

Nicholas the Frenchman general in his Fiery Arrow letter to the Order accused members of losing their way as they migrated from the desert to the city and its allurements. He accused them of following their own disordered desires under the guise of necessary ministry. The reforms of Albi, Mantua, John Soreth, Teresa of Avila, and Touraine continually reminded Carmelites to have one God, and to serve that God with all their heart.

The saints in our tradition knew how hard it is to find and follow the true God, among the many gods offered us. This Presence deep within our lives is met in the world around us. In his Spiritual Canticle poem John of the Cross observes that *"All who are free tell me a thousand graceful things of You..."* (5) Teresa of Avila counseled, *"Let creatures speak to you of their maker."*

In our exuberance however, we continually ask of God's creation more than it can be. We regularly pour our heart's desires into some part of God's creation and ask it to be the fulfilment we seek. We ask some part of God's creation to be uncreated. We take a good and ask it to be a god.

The heart, weary from its continual pilgrimage, seeks to settle down and make camp, refusing to go on. It settles down with lesser gods, finding some joy, peace, identity, security or other alleviations of its desires. This short term relief masks a spiritual problem and also a problem in human development. John of the Cross was convinced that when the individual centers on something or someone other than God, the personality eventually becomes dysfunctional.

Such "attachments" create a situation of death. Whatever or whomever I am asking to be my god, my desires' deepest fulfilment, cannot bear the expectation. The idol will begin to crumble under such pressure as I ask it to be my "all." And because we cannot grow past our gods, a lesser god means a lesser human being. Consequently, that to which I am "attached" is dying under my need, and I am dying because my deepest desires can find nothing and no one to match their intensity.

The self-transcending dynamism within our humanity will not allow us to declare that we have "arrived" at journey's end. By declaring a premature victory as we cling to idols, we are engaging in inauthentic self-transcendence. In other words, the heart is no longer free to hear and follow the invitation of the Beloved. This slavery of the heart is the result of disordered desire. The solution, the liberation of the heart, is not accomplished by annihilation of desire but by its reorientation.

Disordered relationship

When our tradition talks about attachments, it does not mean that relationship with the world is a problem. Certainly, sometimes the world is a problem. But we have to relate to the one world we have.

Relating to the world is not the basic problem in attachment; it is *how* we are relating that becomes the problem. Our saints are talking to adults whose heart has been enslaved by someone or something in place of God. It is not necessarily the person or thing that is the problem, but the way we are relating to them, the disordered way our desire or longing is being expressed.

It is immaterial whether the idol is valuable or not. The relationship is the critical factor. An incident in the life of John of the Cross is illustrative. One of John's friars had a simple cross made of palm. John took it from him. The friar had little else, and the cross was certainly not valuable, but John discerned that the friar was clinging to his crude cross in a disordered way. It apparently had become a non-negotiable indicating that the friar's relationship to it was skewed.

John observed that whether the bird is tied by a cord or a thin thread, it is still tied. The heart is enslaved by its idols and no longer free to hear the invitation of the Beloved. John identifies a craving in attachments which makes the person poorly attuned to God. John was convinced that a person becomes like that which she loves. This false god will encourage a false self.

It is important to emphasize that the Carmelite tradition does not advocate withdrawal from the world. It is advocating a right relationship with God's world. Without interpretation, Carmel could be understood to be saying that involvement with the world is a hindrance to relationship with God. On the contrary, it is in God's world that God is met.

The Carmelite tradition is addressing those whose hearts have gone out to the world seeking fulfilment and have become scattered and fragmented in their search. Pouring their heart's desires into possessions and relationships which cannot meet the intensity of these desires, the Christian begins to experience an impasse in life. It is a deteriorating situation. The world the Christian is clutching so frantically is having life squeezed out of it by the expectations. And the Christian is being conformed to idols, not transformed into God.

A contemporary theme related to our traditional theme of attachment is addiction. We are coming to realize that we are all addicted in one way or another, and that only God's grace can free us from our addictions. One can be addicted to obviously destructive things, but one can also be addicted to the church, addicted to the Pope, addicted to religious practices, even addicted to Carmel, and addicted to God as we create God to be.

In other words, we can ask part of God's creation to be uncreated, to be the nourishment for the deepest hungers within us as individuals and as a people. We are asking from God's creation what only God can give. And our tradition insists that *nada* (nothing), no part of God's creation, can be substituted for God. Only the one who is *nada* (no thing, yet everything) can be sufficient food for our hunger.

When John of the Cross drew a stylized mountain to picture the journey of transformation he drew three paths up the mountain. The two outside paths, one of worldly goods, the other of spiritual goods, did not reach the top. Only the middle path of the *nadas* attained the summit of Carmel. He amplified his teaching in the picture with several lines of text at the bottom. The lines of the text were variations of the theme, "to possess all, possess nothing."

The text at the bottom of the picture gives insight into John's basic understanding of the spiritual journey. He agrees that we are made to possess all, know all, be all, etc. But he also understands that we will never have all if we ask any part of God's creation to be sufficient for these hungers. His counsel to possess nothing in order to possess all is a cryptic encouragement to never ask some thing (some part of God's creation) to be all. Only the one who is no-thing can be our All.

Such asceticism sounds difficult unless one understands that John is addressing men and women who have tried the other paths in life for fulfilment. Their hearts have gone out in search of the one who loved them and they have become enmeshed in life with hearts broken and scattered. John's counsels are words of life for people dying for lack of proper nourishment. He is pointing out the path of life for pilgrims who have lost their way.

A prophetic role

One writer suggested that the Carmelite vocation is to be suspended between heaven and earth, finding no support in either place. That is a rather dramatic way of saying that ultimately our faith, our confidence and trust in God may have to be its own support, and God leads us beyond all of our earthly and spiritual constructs. At the end of her life, Thérèse of Lisieux found her lifelong hope for heaven mocking her. John of the Cross reminded us of St. Paul's observations: *if we already have what we hope for, it is not hope; hope is in what we do not possess.* The spirituality of John of the Cross has been described as a continual hermeneutic on the nature of God.

Does this suspicion of human intentions and constructs make Carmelites eternally curmudgeons? Or does it allow us to bring a sharp critique regarding the human heart and its idol-making propensity? Is it not actually a ministry of liberation, freeing us from all the ways we enslave ourselves and give ourselves away to idols? Is not the Carmelite critique a challenge to not cling to anything, to not make anything center in one's life, other than the Mystery who haunts our lives. And in that purity of heart, really only achieved by God's spirit, are we able to love others well and live in this world wisely. The Carmelite challenge is to cooperate with God's love, often dark, which is enlivening and healing us.

This continual listening for the approach of God, in the middle of all the words and structures we have constructed, is a prophetic task for Carmel. Which God are we to follow? The gods of our addictions? The gods of ideologies and limited theologies? The gods of oppressive economic and political systems? The gods of all the "isms" of our time? Or is our God the God who transforms, heals, liberates, enlivens?

Archbishop Oscar Romero was a traditional, careful, studious cleric. He was a good man, reserved, pious, prayerful. But his conversion came when he saw another face of Christ, a face somewhat different from the Christ of his piety and prayer, a face somewhat different from his theology. It was the face of Christ in the face of the people of El Salvador; it was the face of Christ truly incarnated in history and finding its outlines in the struggles of his people. Romero said,

> *"We learn to see the face of Christ – the face of Christ that also is the face of a suffering human being, the face of the crucified, the face of the poor, the face of a saint, and the face of every person and we love each one with the criteria with which we will be judged: "I was hungry and you gave me to eat."* (6)

The idols of our times are not just personal loves and possessions, but are especially the idols of power, prestige, control, and dominance which leave most of humankind looking in at the banquet of life. Romero commented:

> *"The poor person is the one who has been converted to God and puts all his faith in him, and the rich person is one who has not been converted to God and puts his confidence in idols: money, power, material things ...Our work should be directed toward converting ourselves and all people to this authentic meaning of poverty."* (7)

Many of our provinces have participated in confronting the idols of our times through liberation movements in many areas of the world, including the Philippines, Latin America, North America, Africa, Indonesia, and eastern Europe. Today, the inequities between north and south often point to idols of "isms" which keep a majority of the world in a marginated condition.

Summary

The hungers of our heart send us into the world seeking nourishment. In many ways we ask the world, "Have you seen the one who did this to my heart, causing it to ache?" Our heart finds itself scattered over the landscape as we ask each person and each possession and each activity to tell us more about the Mystery at the core of our lives.

So enamored by the messengers of God, the soul mistakes them for God. We take the good things of God and ask that they be god. The heart, tired of its pilgrimage, seeks to settle down and make a home. It pours its deepest desires into relationships, possessions, plans, activities, goals, and asks that they bring fulfilment to our deepest hungers. We ask too much from them and they begin to crumble under our expectations. Over and over the Carmelite saints remind us that only God is sufficient food for the hungers of the heart.

Questions for reflection:

- What are the idols, the non-negotiables, that have become part of my life? What are those things without which I cannot go on? Am I hurting them by clinging so tightly to them?

- Where and how have I become unfree in life? Am I unfree to follow my deepest desires? Am I unfree to hear God's call into God's future, which is dark to me? Am I unfree to hear my community's needs?

- Have I, unconsciously, been building my kingdom rather than watching for the reign of God? Have I, without being aware of it, removed God from the center of my life and placed in that center *my* noble goals, *my* prophetic work, *my* understanding of the demands of the kingdom? Have I slowly over the years forgotten to ask, "What does God want?"

- Have the passions which brought me to Carmel been domesticated and left to wither? Have I become compulsively active, perhaps becoming more a functionary of an institution rather than a disciple of the Lord?

A LISTENING HEART
The contemplative life

God, always already there

One of the most impressive messages from our Carmelite saints, has been the realization that God loves us first, as we are. Thinking they were looking for an absent God and that life was a pursuit of God, they returned from their efforts testifying that God had been pursuing them all along. That the story of our lives is not our search for God, but God's desire for, and pursuit of, us. The hungers of our heart, the desire that we are, is the result of God first desiring us and coming to us in love. In time, we may be so transformed that we live with a consonance of desire, our human desire fully participating in God's desire.

> *On one occasion, Teresa of Avila heard these words in prayer: "Seek yourself in me!" She asked a number of her friends and directors in Avila the meaning of "Seek yourself in me!" Among the respondents were a lay spiritual director, Francisco de Salcedo, her brother Lorenzo de Cepeda, and John of the Cross. These gentlemen met to discuss their responses but Teresa was absent. So they sent their replies to her.*

> *In imitation of academic sparring sometimes practiced in the schools, Teresa playfully deter-*

mined to find fault with each answer and gently mock it. We do not have their responses, but we do have her rejections of their answers. One respondent, Francisco de Salcedo, quoted St. Paul frequently, and then closed his response with a humble statement about having "written stupidities." Teresa then chastised him for characterizing the words of St. Paul as "stupidities." She said she had a mind to hand him over to the Inquisition.

John of the Cross must have responded that "Seek yourself in me" required that she be dead to the world in order to seek herself in God. Teresa's answer to him was a prayer to be saved from people as spiritual as John of the Cross. His answer was good for members of the Company of Jesus, she said, but not for those she had in mind. Life is not long enough if we have to die to the world before we find God. Teresa pointed to the gospels and observed that Mary Magdalene was not dead to the world before she met Jesus; nor was the Canaanite woman dead to the world before she asked for crumbs from the table. And the Samaritan woman had not died to the world before encountering Jesus at the well. She was who she was and Jesus accepted her. Teresa closed her response to John of the Cross by thanking him for answering what she did not ask! (8)

Teresa's point is, God meets us and accepts us where we are in our lives. We have been accepted all along. The challenge for us is to accept the acceptance, and allow that accepting Presence to change us. The reality of that embrace is the basis for our prayer. To pray, then, is to step trustingly into that relationship as the foundation of our lives. It is easy to talk about, but very difficulty to live day by day.

One theologian summed up Teresa's message in this way: a faithful and perduring attentiveness to our depths and center is the best cooperation we can give to God who is reorienting our life.

Lured by love

The Carmelite tradition can be misread. Carmel could easily appear to be saying to people that a rigorous asceticism will achieve union with God; that the idols of our lives can be toppled with our courageous efforts and isolated, rugged living. When in fact, Carmel's message to people is the necessity for God's grace, and the good news that grace is always available. All we need do is open our lives to it.

In *The Ascent of Mount Carmel* John of the Cross offers several counsels for detaching from the idols which have fooled us into their service. The counsels at first seem unnecessarily restrictive and even imbalanced. But John is quick to point out that willpower and asceticism alone cannot free the heart enslaved to idols. The idol, at least, is providing some nourishment for the heart hungering for God. The idol perhaps is providing some joy, some identity, some security to the famished pilgrim. On its own, the heart is not going to be able to tear itself away from this nourishment and go into an affective vacuum and await the Lord.

John testifies that it is only when the heart has a better offer can it let go of what it has been clinging to for dear life. Only when God enters a life and kindles a love deep in the person that lures the person past lesser loves can a person open his or her grasp of idols. With the invitation of such a love then, what was impossible before (letting go of one's grasp on idols) becomes gently possible as idols melt away. The heart then is going from love to love. Because John is convinced that God is the soul's center, the task is not to find a distant God but to awake to the reality of a God who is "always already there."

"Everything is a grace," said Thérèse of Lisieux. She expressed this conviction while dying of tuberculosis, surrounded by a spir-

ituality which deeply mistrusted human nature, believed that we had to merit God's love, and called for "victim souls" to appease God's wrath. Nonetheless, when told she could no longer receive Holy Communion, she simply said it was a grace when she could receive, and now that she cannot receive, it is still a grace. *"Everything is a grace!"*

Thérèse was convinced that God was always present to her, that God loved her, and that this love was freely given; it was absolutely unmerited by her. When speaking of merit, she simply said *"I have none."*

Thérèse knew about God's justice, and she was aware that devout people often offered themselves as victims to that justice so that sinners may be spared and God appeased. This God was not familiar to Thérèse. None of the faces of God in her life demanded appeasement, not her mother, or her father, not Pauline, nor Celine, nor Marie, not the God the Hebrew Bible who loved little ones, not Jesus who called little ones to him, not the Beloved in the *Song of Songs* or in the poetry of John of the Cross. She believed that God is just, but that this justice will be well aware of our littleness.

Thérèse of Lisieux was once described as *Vatican II in miniature.* The recent attention paid to her message reminds us that priority should be given not to our merits and efforts, but to living with confidence and trust. Thérèse begins her autobiography with St. Paul's words to the Romans: *"So it depends not on human will or exertion, but on God who shows mercy."* (9)

Thérèse anticipated today's theology which understands grace as uncreated grace, the loving, healing presence of the Father, Son, and Spirit. When we speak of contemplation, we are simply encouraging an openness to this freely given love. God is continually coming toward us inviting us more deeply into our lives, into a wider freedom, and into a loving relationship. Contemplation is being open to that transforming love, no matter how it is approaching.

Contemplation re-focused

One of the recent developments in the understanding of the Carmelite charism has been the re-locating of contemplation among our priorities. We had always spoken about prayer, community, and ministry as the three corners of our charism. Contemplation was seen as a higher or deeper form of prayer and, at times in our history, ministry and contemplation appeared to be in competition. However, here is a description of contemplation found in the Carmelite Order's recent document on formation:

> *"...a progressive and continual transformation in Christ worked in us by the Spirit, by which God attracts us toward Himself by means of an interior process which leads from a dispersed periphery of life to the more interior cell of our being, where He dwells and unites us to Himself."* (10)

We are understanding now that contemplation is an activity which grounds and links prayer, community, and ministry. The door is prayer, but God's love is offered us in various ways in those realities of our lives and one can enter into this contemplative openness to God, in other words live a life of authentic faith, hope, and love, through any of those three avenues. They are not pitted one against another, but they are windows to the transcendent reality at the depth of our lives and offer contact with that Mystery.

It is important to stress this perspective because Carmel has had 800 years of ministry in response to the Church and God's people, and, God-willing, will have many more centuries of unselfish service. And none of it is inimical to a contemplative life. Many a Carmelite has been transformed into a more loving person through engagement with God's people in various ministries.

Archbishop Romero was transformed and converted by God's love not only in the solitude of his prayer, but in his engagement with the Lord in history, in the messy efforts of the people to find their place at the banquet of life. Contemplation should be the deepest source of compassion for our world. The contemplative is one who has been led into the absolute poverty and powerlessness of a soul apart from God. The contemplative learns to wait in hope with all who wait in hope for God's mercy. In this contemplative listening one learns to say, "We poor!"

Our contemplative living, our openness to God's love coming toward us in good times and bad is the gift we can give to others. What happened in the lives of Carmel's saints, what is happening in the lives of Carmelites today, is happening in everyone's life. We witness best by keeping a focus on who we are: a contemplative fraternity living in the midst of the people.

Speaking to the Order's General Congregation in 1999 a German Carmelite stressed this contemplative charism:

> *"I strongly believe that our first task is to put quite a bit of our energy, time, and personal talents and qualities into this process of a growing relationship with the God of life and love. Our personal human and spiritual growth as well as our future as an Order depend on how much we as individuals and communities yield to and develop this intimate friendship with God so that he can transform us according to the image of Christ, acting through us for the sake of the Church and the world."* (11)

Summary

The story of the Beloved coming toward the lover to lure her heart into a deep union is the archetypal story Carmelites have rehearsed time and time again. Our lives cannot be wrestled into submission unless led by love. We cannot release our grasp on our idols unless God kindles a deeper love in the soul. The heart then has somewhere to go and can trustingly let go of its attachments, its addictions, its idols. God's love, always present and offered, lures the heart into God's wilderness, *"deeper into the thicket,"* (12) and there encounters the suffering of the world. Our contemplative stance does not remove us from the world's cares but opens us to the full force of its struggle.

Questions for reflection:

- Like "a watch in the night," do I keep alert to the approach of God's love? Where in my life am I called to a deeper listening? Where are the continual challenges to my mind and heart? Are these challenges invitations to surrender more deeply to God's transforming love?

- Among the signs of God's love at work are a growing trust in the mercy of God, and a growing freedom from what enslaves the heart. Do I experience that greater trust? Am I aware of a greater freedom? Have I really surrendered myself to the Mystery at the core of my life, or do I continue to struggle to secure my own existence?

- Have I seen the face of Christ in the face of the people I serve? Can I recognize the invitation of God's transforming love as it approaches cloaked in a culture?

- In my community and in my ministry, how can I help create conditions for a "listening heart"?

A TROUBLED HEART
The tragic in life

The sorrows of humanity

Part of the appeal of the Carmelite tradition is its honest wrestling with the problems and dark forces that attack the body and spirit. Carmel does not avoid the tragic in life but deals with it directly. Suffering is such a major part of people's experience that a spirituality which does not acknowledge the suffering will be ignored. Carmel's saints deeply shared in the difficulties of life.

Edith Stein and Titus Brandsma experienced the depth of human cruelty and inexplicable evil. Thérèse of Lisieux, in her short, hidden life, experienced a surprising amount of suffering. Teresa of Avila knew the damage caused by warfare both outside and inside her soul. The heavy reputation of John of the Cross, his very name, and his image of the *"dark night"* speak of a spirituality that is serious about coming to terms with the dark side of life. Think, too, about the first Carmelites who went to the periphery of society and there, without distractions, opened their lives to the inner warfare of evil and good spirits.

People are drawn to a spirituality which finds words for their deepest sorrows, yet offers hope in the heart of these dark times. Carmel's saints, though of differing centuries and cultures, entered into the common sorrows of humanity. A pilgrim in any era can relate to the sufferings of Carmel's saints and call on them as companions in the valley of sorrows. It is good to rehearse their difficulties.

For example, many people today can identify with the problems of Thérèse of Lisieux. As a child Thérèse experienced the loss not only of her real mother, but also of subsequent "mothers" who cared for her. Her fragile psyche knew the sufferings of neuroticism and the debilitation of psychosomatic illness. She helplessly watched the mental deterioration and eventual institutionalization of her father, an heroic figure in her life. She experienced Carmel as a desert and in her final physical and psychological illness she knew the temptation to suicide. Devotees of Thérèse have never been fooled by the sweet exterior. They recognized in her a fellow sufferer who knew by experience just how difficult life can be. And yet, she testified to a love present in it all which will not fail.

Thérèse expressed a life-long desire to suffer. It had a mysterious attraction for her, which would be suspect had she not related it to love. From the time she entered Carmel, Thérèse began to experience dryness in prayer and remained in this condition throughout the rest of her brief time in Carmel. And, most amazingly, her autobiography with its especially appealing manuscript "B" was written while Thérèse was suffering an extremely dark night of the spirit when all was in doubt. The idea of heaven, which had been her life-long inspiration, was mocking her for her belief in it. Cognitively and affectively she had no assurance regarding the direction in her life. Meanwhile she was writing the beautiful passages about being love in the heart of the church, and sending inspiring letters to her missionary brothers.

Thérèse was undergoing her own transformation in the furnace of a dark love. All she had left was the core of faith, confidence and love. When she encourages us to have trust and to believe that *"everything is a grace"* she does so not from a position of tangible delights in the loving presence of God but from an experience of God's absence and the taunts of her own mind. Cardinal Daneels wondered if Thérèse could not be called the "Doctor of

Hope" because of her testimony to the human possibility to continue on in life when all the props have been removed.

The dark love of God

Teresa of Avila warned that the battles within our fragile psyches are much more difficult than the wars outside us. Teresa had numerous obstacles to overcome in her reform. She had to contend with opponents of her reform, purchase appropriate buildings for her communities, hire men to renovate them, raise funds for their maintenance, recruit community members, relate to various ecclesiastics, not all of whom were supportive, travel the difficult roads of Spain in extreme conditions, and at times deal with litigation in the courts.

However, she reported, these battles did not compare with the battles waged within her soul as she prayerfully attended to her depths. *… Hearing His voice is a greater trial than not hearing it.* (13) One would assume, Teresa mused, that *going within oneself* would be like going home; that the wars outside are one thing, but within the soul all is harmonious. However, she reported that she went within herself, and found she was at war with herself.

Prayer throws light on previously unexamined corners of the soul. Compulsions, addictions, inauthentic ways of living, false selves, and false gods all become apparent as the person becomes grounded in truth. This uncomfortable experience can lead to fear and faintheartedness, and a temptation to abandon the journey. Teresa's call for courage and determination in the pursuit of a prayer life are not overly-dramatic. What the soul needs, Teresa wrote, is self-knowledge. And the door to self-knowledge, the door to the interior castle, is prayer and reflection.

Without a prayerful effort, we remain hopelessly locked on the periphery of our lives asking others and God's creation to tell us what only God can tell us, that is, who we are. Without a true center emerging in our lives we live with many "centers," fragmented and scattered, asking each to fulfil our heart's desires. The painful battle to enter within oneself in prayer is the only antidote to a sure death locked in the embrace of one's idols.

Modern readers can sympathize with Teresa as she rehearses a catalogue of difficulties in her life, including being overly praised and being unfairly criticized; she suffered the contradiction of good men who thought her prayer experiences were from the devil; and daily she dealt with poor health.

But a most difficult experience arose just when her relationship with the Lord was the most intimate. She began to question her entire journey and wondered if it were rooted in her imagination rather than the reality of God's presence in her life. Had she simply imagined that God had been good to her in the past? Had she been good in the past or simply made it up? In other words, just when the friendship with God would be expected to be on solid ground, the question flares up, *Is there anybody home at the center?* Having given one's life and best energy to the following of her perceived call, she began to wonder if it were all an illusion.

Another way the question has been asked is, *Is the ultimate gracious?* Is whatever or whomever it is all about for us? Or are we a useless passion? Are the immense desires of our hearts, the hungers of our soul, meant to be ultimately frustrated? Or is there a reality, a love awaiting us equal to our yearning? These questions get to the heart of the human journey.

Time and perseverance, and God's grace, eventually answered Teresa's doubts. She later reports the absence of such gnawing doubts and the surety of a profound, but not preoccupying, relationship with the Lord. But even in that condition she identifies as the "spiritual marriage" she still reports that she trusts suffering more. Not as hard on herself as when she was locked out of herself and locked into the periphery of her life, she still knew that the disciple of Jesus would carry the cross, and through the cross life would emerge. She did not artificially construct crosses in her life, but she did not dodge the crosses life presents. She had learned to trust in the sometimes dark love of God.

Dark nights

The dark night metaphor of John of the Cross reminds us that the experience of God's love is not always a peak experience of the unity of all creation. In the dark night God's love approaches in a way which seems to negate us. In the night God seems over against us. Nothing in the loves is dark or destructive, John maintains, but because of who we are and the purification we need the love is experienced as dark.

John provides an especially powerful description of times in life when consolations evaporate and prayer is all but impossible. Desire is still present but it has exhausted itself looking for relief from its idols. Theologian Karl Rahner commented that all symphonies in life remain unfinished. In every relationship, in every possession an incompleteness will eventually surface. This frustration of desire and the lure of something more or beyond is the unease caused by God's continual invitation into deeper union.

When "gods" die in the night, the personality goes into an eclipse. Psychologist Carl Jung' observed that he could not distinguish god-symbols from self-symbols. When an individual loses her god-symbol the personality begins to disintegrate. This dark condition lasts until a new god-symbol emerges or a new relationship develops with the old god-symbol.

The counsel of John of the Cross during these crises in life is most helpful. He assures us that God's love is somewhere present in the debris of our life, but it will not be experienced as love initially. John encourages patience, trust, and perseverance. This loving activity of God is freeing us from idols and restoring health to the soul. "Gods" are dying in the night and the soul needs to undergo a grieving process. The wrong path would be to artificially solve or heal the condition, or deny it altogether. John encourages facing the condition, entering into it with patience, and there, where the heart is struggling hardest, to be alert for the approach of love. John calls for a "loving attentiveness" in the dark; it is time to be a watch in the night. Contemplation is an openness to God's transforming love, especially when it approaches in such a disguised manner.

An intense experience which John calls the night of the spirit is simultaneously a powerful experience of our sinfulness, the finiteness of our human condition, and God's ever-emerging transcendence. While in this condition, words are meaningless. John writes it is time to *put one's mouth in the dust.* All one can do is the next loving thing which presents itself. In this desert the pilgrim continues the journey in life, relying only on the guidance of a truly biblical faith. John is convinced that only this purified faith is the context for a proper relationship with God. As with Thérèse of Lisieux's disappearing thought of heaven, the pilgrim no longer possess the object of her hope, and is reminded that hope is in what we do not possess.

John's writings do not wallow in suffering. His poetry, and their commentaries, are all written from the other side of the struggles. The night has become an illuminating experience and a truer guide than day. The flame which once burned now cauterizes and heals. And the absence which drove him in search of the Beloved has revealed a compassionate Presence hidden within his longing.

A new spirituality

Contemporary Carmel's witnesses to a faith maintained in the midst of abject suffering are the concentration camp victims, Titus Brandsma and Edith Stein. Brandsma resisted Nazi propaganda and Stein identified with her persecuted people. They were caught in the undertow of the 20th century's powerful expression of societal evil. In their experience of being stripped of all security and support these Carmelites witnessed to the possibility of a faith, hope, and love lived in the bleakest of conditions. In recognizing their witness the Church confirms the authenticity of their lives and places them among those who have risked everything in their following of Christ. The Rule of Carmel leads to various forms of discipleship, but all forms eventually embrace the Cross.

The generals of two Carmelite orders called for a *"new spirituality"* to complement the *"new evangelisation."* Will that new spirituality grow out of Carmel's ever-increasing awareness of the realities people are experiencing around the word? As the face of Carmel changes and new members enter the Order, especially from populous, poor countries, the situation of the world's masses is brought to the first-world's doorstep. The internationality of the Order and international bonds forged in the family of Carmel give us a unique opportunity to hear the Spirit in many diverse contexts, and the opportunity to be challenged to respond.

John Paul II amplified John of the Cross' image of the dark night to include the modern world's sufferings:

> *"Our age has known times of anguish which have made us understand this expression better and which have furthermore given it a kind of collective character. Our age speaks of the silence or absence of God. It has known so many calamities, so much suffering inflicted by wars and by the destruction of so many innocent beings. The term dark night is now used of all of life and not just of a phase of the spiritual journey. The Saint's doctrine is now invoked in response to this unfathomable mystery of human suffering.*

> *I refer to this specific world of suffering... Physical, moral and spiritual suffering, like sickness – like the plagues of hunger, like war, injustice, solitude, the lack of meaning in life, the very fragility of human existence, the sorrowful knowledge of sin, the seeming absence of God – are for the believer all purifying experiences which might be called night of faith.*

> *To this experience St. John of the Cross has given the symbolic and evocative name dark night, and he makes it refer explicitly to the plight and obscurity of the mystery of faith. He does not try to give to the appalling problem of suffering an answer in the speculative order; but in the light of*

SEASONS OF THE HEART

> *the Scripture and of experience he discovers and*
> *sifts out something of the marvellous transforma-*
> *tion which God effects in the darkness, since 'He*
> *knows how to draw good from evil so wisely and*
> *beautifully' (Cant. B 23:5). In the final analysis,*
> *we are faced with living the mystery of death and*
> *resurrection in Christ in all truth.* (14)"

Summary

Carmel has no answer for the mystery of evil. But Carmel has
travelled the hard road and offers a word of hope for the tearful
pilgrim. Deep sorrow and experiences of the tragic are part of
everyone's life. The limitations of our human condition and the
destructive forces loose in the world often assault our faith.
Despite all evidence to the contrary, Carmel testifies that God's
love is always present in the debris of our lives.

Carmel brings a particularly powerful analysis of the impact of
God's love on the human spirit and personality. Invited into an
ever-deeper relationship, the pilgrim is challenged to let go of all
supports and walk trustingly into God's future. A Christian often
experiences assaults on both spirit and psyche as he or she is
accommodated to the divine milieu. Carmel offers expressive language and images for these sufferings, and is most eloquent in
urging a silent vigil for God's approach.

Carmel's saints trusted suffering, and often expressed a yearning
to bear the cross in their discipleship. However, this desire for suffering is most meaningful in the context of a loving response to
God's initiatives. The suffering of Jesus on the cross was born
because of love, not because of a love of suffering.

Questions for reflection:

- What has been my experience of walking a dark way? Have
  I been able to let go of known paths to be led by a way not
  of my choosing? What, particularly, was most helpful?

- How do I proceed when the way is not clear?

- What solace or guidance does Carmel offer to people living in distressing situations?

- How should the Order respond to the "dark night" suffered by many peoples in the world? Could this be part of the "new spirituality" urged by the Carmelite and Discalced Carmelite generals?

A PURE HEART
Transformation of Desire

Union with God

Carmelite spirituality has frequently been presented as a "high" spirituality, a rarefied spirituality for the chosen few. It is often presented as soaring ecstatic unions, or dramatic sufferings more intense than the usual troubles in life. Images come to mind of Bernini's statue of Teresa's "transverberation," her vision of being pierced by a golden dart with all the accompanying ecstasy and agony.

John of the Cross' stark drawing of Christ on the Cross, from the perspective of the Father looking down on his crucified Son, evokes the unremitting single-mindedness of the saint. Or one thinks of John's drawing showing the way up Mount Carmel. The paths of material and spiritual possessions do not reach the top; only the middle path of the nadas opens to the top where God is *nada* and *todo* (no thing, yet everything!). Carmel seems to represent an heroic, even epic journey to God. And it is only for experienced mountaineers who dare scale its heights.

If the ascent of Mount Carmel is such an epic feat, what are we ordinary Carmelites doing here? Do we sometimes feel we are guardians of a tradition we have never really experienced? Do we feel that we often are reporting second hand accounts of the land that is Carmel, but have never really been there ourselves? As a result of our transformation in love, "We become god!" John of the Cross boldly proclaims. How rare is this divinisation celebrated in our tradition?

An awakening

John uses another image for the journey, besides traveling through a night or climbing a mountain. He writes that *"The soul's center is God"* and that our journey in life is to that center. (15) But, instead of envisioning a distant center requiring an arduous journey, John says that even with *one degree of love* we are in the center! With one degree of desire, of yearning, of hope, no matter how inarticulate, we are in the center.

Our theology today reinforces John's observation. Strictly speaking, there is no natural world. It is a graced world, from the beginning, creation and redemption going hand in hand. In other words, our lives are permeated with the loving, enlivening, healing presence of God, uncreated grace. Instead of searching for a hidden center, the center has come to us.

So, what is the journey? The journey, said John, is to go deeper into God. But we are in union with God all the way; divinisation is a continual process. So, the goal described by our Carmelite authors is one taking place in each soul who only feebly desires more.

"And now you awake in my heart, where in secret you dwelt all along," wrote John of the Cross. But in his commentary he corrects himself and says it was not *"you"* who awoke, but it was I who awoke to the love always present and continually offered me. This awakening, and the difference it makes in a person's life, is Carmel's call. A conclusion we could draw is that many, many Carmelites and certainly others as well reach the so-called "heights" of Carmel. The heights are approached, not when someone drops off their pew in a swoon, but when a life more and more is expressing God's will.

To want what God wants

The purpose of prayer is conformity with God's will, wrote Teresa of Avila. The prayerful person is more and more in union with God and this union is expressed in the individual more and more wanting what God wants. We do not get tougher ascetically and thereby wrestle our will into submitting to God's will. No, God's love lures us into a transformation of our desire so that we desire what God desires; we want what God wants. John reported, *"What you desire me to ask for, I ask for; and what you do not desire, I do not desire, nor can I, nor does it even enter my mind to desire it."* (16)

Divinization is the gradual participation in God's knowing and loving. The pilgrim is so transformed that all their ways of living become expressive of God's will. If we may interpret Jesus as saying that God's will is the well-being of humanity, then the prayerful person is more and more living in a way which furthers that well-being. In other words, the transformed, divinized person is living in a way which cooperates with God's present and coming reign.

These people are hard to identify. Meister Eckhart warns us that someone living from their center very naturally lives in accord with God's will. He says while others fast, they are eating; while others keep vigil, they are asleep; and while others pray, they are silent. After all, what is the purpose of the vigil, the prayer, the fasting, if not to live out of the soul's center, which is God. Of course, he is exaggerating to make a point since our pilgrimage is never finished this side of death. The point, I take it, is the absolute humanness of the transformed person.

Teresa tells us that these people are not even continually conscious of their spiritual life. Interiority becomes less and less an object of focus. Not even God preoccupies them, because in all the ways they are living they are expressing their relationship with God. The goal was never to be a contemplative, or a saint, or to have a spiritual life. The goal was always to want what God wants, in a consonance of desire.

In the conclusion of the Carmelite Rule, Albert, Patriarch of Jerusalem and the law-giver, writes *"Here then are a few points I have written down to provide you with a standard of conduct to live up to; but our Lord, at his Second Coming will reward anyone who does more than he is obliged to do."* (17) Kees Waaijman of the Brandsma Institute in Nijmegen sees this statement as a clear allusion to the Good Samaritan story. The Carmelite is placed in the role of innkeeper. His plans and orderly house are upset when a stranger brings a beaten man to be cared for. The stranger asks the innkeeper to take care of the beaten man, and *if the innkeeper incurs further expense, i.e. does more,* the stranger will compensate him when he returns.

The stranger, Christ, asks the Carmelite to take care of His people in His absence. The guest is unexpected, the order of the house is disturbed. But the innkeeper dutifully takes care of the wounded person, perhaps without emotional investment or ego-involvement, and maybe with very little satisfaction. Kees concludes that all real giving is essentially dark. The Presence met deep in Carmelite hearts is a night that guides, a flame that heals, an absence that reveals.

Friars need make no apologies for not being true Carmelites. Our spirituality is not about heroic asceticism; it is about God's all-conquering love, a love that has touched every heart and made it ache; otherwise we would not be here.

Realizing that we are naturally at home on the heights of Carmel, or better, in the arms of God, and still always in need of God's mercy, our spiritual ministry is to make available Carmel's tradition to help our brothers and sisters "see" and "hear" the presence of God in their own lives.

In order to tend this flame in others, it seems right that we will have come to terms with it in our own lives. If we listen to our hearts, we will know the hearts of the people with whom we live and minister. Dust off any Carmelite vocation and you will usually find a glowing ember waiting to be fanned into a flame, a flame that yearns for wholeness, peace, security, joy, unity, and that finds its best expression in service of our brothers and sisters. That is why we came. That is why we stay.

Summary

"Entering Carmel" is not simply a matter of entering a building, joining a community, and taking on a ministry, whether of prayer or apostolic mission. It is that, certainly, but *"entering Carmel"* is also entering a drama playing out deep within every human life. That drama of the human spirit encountered by God's Spirit is essentially inexpressible.

Carmelites are explorers of an inner place of intimacy with God, a fine point of the human spirit where it is addressed by Mystery. Carmel honors that pristine, privileged relationship between creature and Creator. Carmelite mystics have used bridal imagery and, regularly, the love story of the *Song of Songs* to capture the intimacy of this encounter. The landscape of the *Song* begins to give shape to the "land of Carmel."

The purpose of prayer is conformity with God's will, writes Teresa of Avila. In this relationship the desires of the pilgrim are transformed so that more and more the life of a Christian is expressing desires which are in accord with God's desire. If we may describe the goal of God's desire as the well-being of humanity, then the transformed Christian is living in a manner which naturally cooperates with the reign of God.

Questions for reflection:

- Who are the truly holy people in my experience? What do they look like?

- Do I understand the spiritual life as an heroic ascent, or an awakening to a love always offered from the core of my being?

- Am I able to trust, in practical ways, that God's love is freely given, unable to be earned? Are there subtle ways I try to guarantee my worth?

- "Relax, it has been done!" said one theologian of grace. What might that expression mean?

NOTES

1. Teresa of Avila, *The Book of Her Life in The Collected Works of St. Teresa of Avila,* 1, trans. Kieran Kavanaugh, O.C.D., and Otilio Rodriguez, O.C.D. (Washington, D.C.: ICS Publications, 1987), chap. 8, no. 12.

2. Ronald Rolheiser, *The Holy Longing* (New York: Doubleday, 1999), 27.

3. Teresa of Avila, *The Way of Perfection,* chap. 19, no. 2.

4. John of the Cross, "The Spiritual Canticle," in *The Collected Works of St. John of the Cross,* trans. Kieran Kavanaugh, O.C.D. and Otilio Rodriguez, O.C.D. (Washington D.C.: ICS Publications, 1991), stanza 1.

5. John of the Cross, *Spiritual Canticle,* st. 7.

6. Marie Dennis, Renny Golden, Scott Wright, *Oscar Romero* (Maryknoll: Orbis Books, 2000), 19.

7. *Ibid.,* 28.

8. Teresa of Avila, *A Satirical Critique in The Collected Works of St. Teresa of Avila,* 3, 359-362.

9. Romans, 9, 16.

10. *Ratio Institutionis Vitae Carmelitanae,* #27.

11. Gunter Benker, "Open to the Future of God" in *The Mission of Carmel for the Third Millennium* (Melbourne: Carmelite Communications, 1999), 51.

12. John of the Cross, *Spiritual Canticle,* st. 36.

13. Teresa of Avila, *The Interior Castle,* The Second Dwelling Places, chap. 1, no. 2.

14. *Master in Faith*, Apostolic Letter of John Paul II in *Walking Side by Side with All Men and Women* (Rome: Institutum Carmelitanum, 1991), 22, 23.

15. John of the Cross, *The Living Flame of Love*, st. 1, number 12.

16. John of the Cross, *The Living Flame of Love*, st. 1, no. 36.

17. *Carmelite Constitutions 1995,* (Rome and Middle Park Victoria, Australia: Carmelite Communications, 1996), 5. The Rule may also be found in John Welch, O.Carm., *The Carmelite Way* (Mahwah, New Jersey: Paulist Press, 1996), 175-181.

Artwork in
Seasons of the Heart

Artist's Reflections
Catherine Martin, O. Carm.

A LONGING HEART
Our desire for God

The rhythm of the heart is interspersed by undefined and scattered sparks of light representing the restless wanderings of the heart as it seeks and yearns for *"something or someone to match the depth of its desire."*

AN ENSLAVED HEART
The worship of false gods

The art shows tension between the center half and outer half of the circle. Surrounding the heart, there appears a thicket-like impasse. The soul struggles between *"the mystery that haunts our lives"* deep within and the bright, alluring distractions of the world's offerings.

A LISTENING HEART
The contemplative life

In the center, the heart is enflamed with God's desire and all embracing love for the soul. The art identifies a trail of light forming the contour of an ear leaning into the depth of mystery, where in contemplation, the heart hears the voice of the Beloved *"and there encounters the sufferings of the world."*

A TROUBLED HEART
The tragic in life

Troubles and the tragic in life weigh heavy upon the soul and the soul is in darkness. *"The pilgrim is challenged to let go of all supports and walk trustingly into God's future."* (This is symbolized by a faint spiral movement through the darkness toward the center). And there in the center, though seemingly obscured and veiled, the light is there, and the heart awaits in *"silent vigil for God's approach."*

A PURE HEART
Transformation of desire

A pure heart is in God's center and lives in God's presence. The presence of God, deep within the heart is *"a night that guides"* (the blue background), *"a flame that heals"* (sun-like flame) and *"an absence that reveals"* (an open center). The pure heart, the transformed heart finds its best expression in loving service.

COVER ART

Each of the seasons, the longing heart, enslaved heart, listening heart, troubled heart and pure heart is revealed in some way in the ONE HEART.